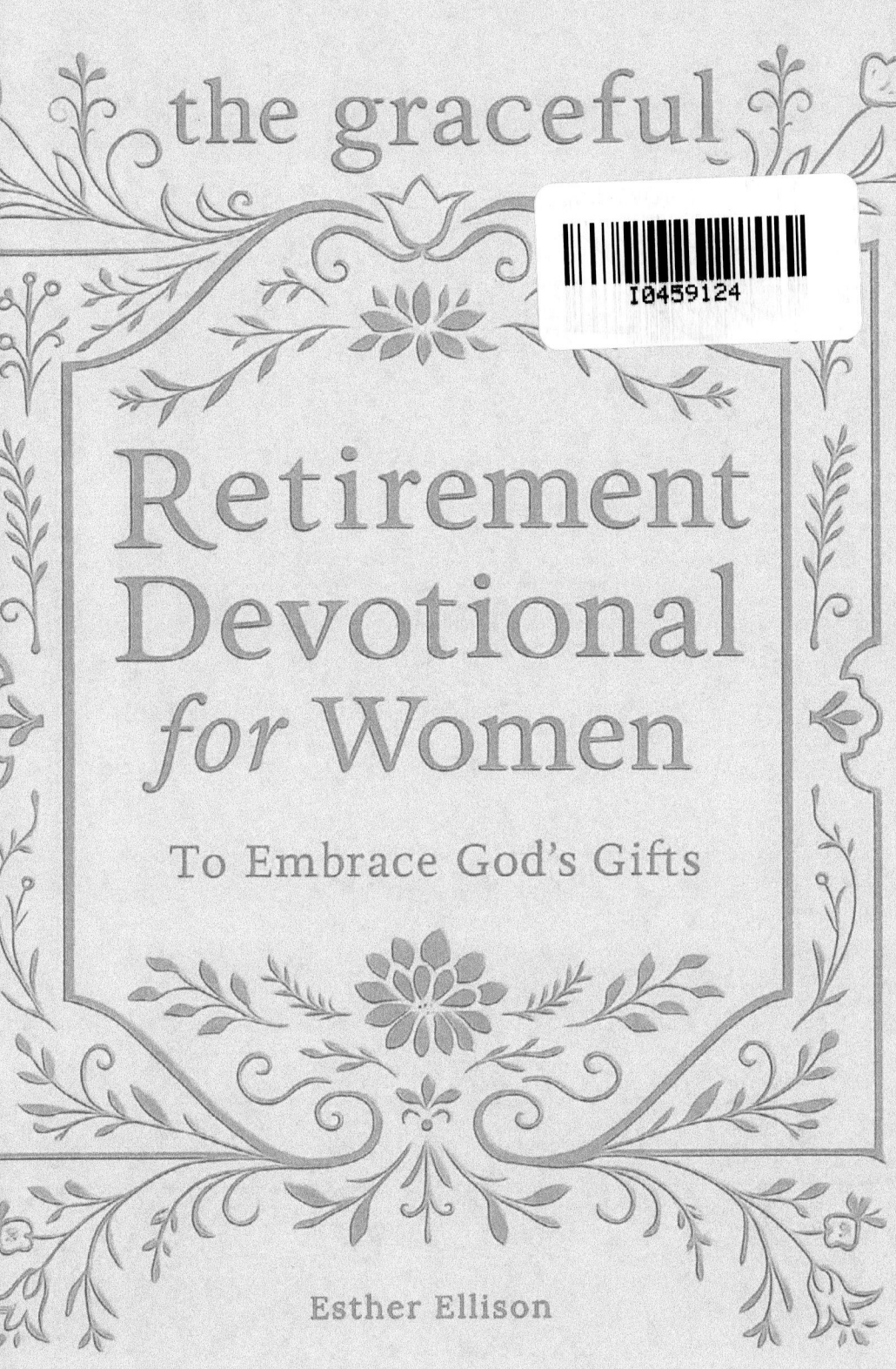

the graceful

Retirement
Devotional
for Women

To Embrace God's Gifts

Esther Ellison

From: _____

To: _____

Note & Date: _____

_____

Table of Contents

Week 1 – New Season, New Mercies......................10

Week 2 – Unhurried Mornings 11

Week 3 – Scripture First 12

Week 4 – Pray Your Calendar 13

Week 5: Sabbath as Delight 14

Week 6: Gratitude Rewires the Day 16

Week 7: Listening in Silence................................18

Week 8: Review and Reset...................................19

Week 9: Beloved, Not Defined by Role 23

Week 10: Strength in Weakness 25

Week 11: Refuse to Live in the Past...................... 26

Week 12: From Fear to Faith...............................27

Week 12: From Fear to Faith............................. 28

Week 13: Joy in the Ordinary............................ 30

Week 14: Wisdom for Decisions 31

Week 15: Worth That Ripens with Age 32

Week 16: Abide to Bear Fruit 33

Week 17: Temple Care....................................... 36

Week 18: Contentment Now 38

Week 19: Trade Anxiety for Prayer 40

Week 20: Simplicity Frees Attention 42

Week 21: Strength for the Journey 43

Week 22: Redeem the Time 45

Week 23: Rest for Your Soul 46

Week 24: Seek First... 49

Week 25: Gifts to Serve 51

Table of Contents

Week 26: Mentor the Next 52

Week 27: Hospitality as Witness 53

Week 28: Create With God................................. 54

Week 29: Pray for Your City 56

Week 30: Faithful Finances 58

Week 31: God Near the Brokenhearted 62

Week 32: From Isolation to Belonging................... 64

Week 33: Grieve with Hope................................ 65

Week 34: Friendship That Heals 66

Week 35: Prayer Partners & Soul-Safe People 67

Week 36: Healthy Boundaries, Gentle No's 68

Week 37: Courage for New Companionship.....69

Week 39: Grandparenting on Purpose 74

Week 40: Pursue Peace 76

Week 41: Cheerful Giver 78

Week 42: Guard Your Eyes and Mind............. 79

Week 43: Love Your Neighbor........................... 81

Week 44: Encourage One Another 82

Week 45: Do Justice, Love Mercy 85

Week 46: Speak Blessing................................. 86

Week 47: Pray Generational Prayers..................... 87

Week 48: Finish What You Start 88

Week 49: Hope Over Fear................................. 89

Week 50: Remember and Give Thanks...................91

Week 51: Open Hands 92

Week 52: Behold, He Makes All Things New 93

Receive   and spread truth 97

Disclaimer and Legal Notice

Grace for the Next Chapter

"I will instruct you and teach you in the way you should go; I will counsel you with my loving eye on you." – Psalm 32:8

The first Monday of retirement felt both freeing and unsettling. I woke up early, just like always, but there was nowhere to be. The house was quiet, the calendar was empty, and I caught myself wondering, Now what?

That morning, I opened my Bible and was reminded that God's Word is a lamp to my feet. I did not need to see the entire road ahead. I only needed to trust Him for the next step. That truth brought peace and helped me realize that my value did not end when my work ended. God was still leading, still speaking, and still working through me.

This devotional was created for women entering this new season of life who long to walk it with peace, gratitude, and purpose. Each week offers:

Stories that feel familiar, marked by both struggle and breakthrough.

Prayers that give words when you are not sure how to begin.

One simple step that makes faith practical and life-giving.

As these weeks unfold, you may notice less tension in your heart, more steadiness with loved ones, and new joy in everyday moments.

If these pages were placed in your hands by someone who cares for you, let it be a reminder of how deeply you are valued. If you chose this book yourself, let it reflect the care you are giving to your own soul. In both cases, may you find here a quiet rhythm of grace: one step, one prayer, one week at a tim

Step 1 — Reset Your Rhythm

(Weeks 1–8)

Week 1 – New Season, New Mercies

"His mercies never come to an end, they are new every morning." – Lamentations 3:22-23

The first Monday after I retired felt strangely loud. No alarm. No rush. Just the clock ticking and sunlight spilling across the kitchen table. I made coffee and stood in the quiet, a little unsure of where to put my hands. For years my mornings were a blur of tasks. Now I had space, and that space felt empty, like a hallway with too many doors.

I sat in my favorite chair and noticed a thin layer of dust on the windowsill. That dust felt like a picture of my soul. I had been busy for so long that stillness felt awkward. Then I remembered this verse. New mercies. Not leftovers. Not scraps from yesterday. Fresh bread laid out, before I even ask.

I whispered, "Lord, I do not know how to do this season." And in that whisper I sensed a gentle nudge. Retirement is not blank. It is a gift already wrapped. The gift is time soaked in mercy. I opened my Bible and read the verse again, slow. My shoulders dropped. I could breathe.

By the second cup of coffee, the room did not feel empty. It felt prepared. Like a table set for two. The insight settled in my heart. Retirement is not empty space. It is newly gifted time that God has already filled with mercy, one morning at a time.

Prayer

Lord, meet me in this new season. Slow my pace so I can see Your gifts. Trade my hurry for trust. Help me notice fresh mercy on my table each morning and receive it with gratitude. Teach me how to live unhurried and present with You. Amen.

Practical Step

Put a Bible and pen beside your chair tonight, then set a 3-minute timer for tomorrow's first quiet.

Week 2 — Unhurried Mornings

"In the morning you hear my voice." – Psalm 5:3

For years my mornings started with a glowing screen. I told myself I was just checking the weather. Ten minutes later I was reading headlines, answering messages, and chasing small fires that did not belong to me. My heart would race before my feet even touched the floor.

One morning I decided to try something different. I cleared a corner of the coffee table and made a tiny tray. Bible. Reading glasses. A small card for notes. A pen that writes smoothly. I set it on my favorite chair like a welcome mat for my soul. The next morning I walked straight to that spot, sat down, and whispered, "Good morning, Lord." No phone. No scroll. Just breath and quiet.

At first the quiet felt like a blank page. Then it felt like a friend. I read one short psalm and spoke to God about what I read. I did not rush to be deep. I simply showed up. The habit began before the habit, with a prepared place and a short plan. The tray told my brain what to do. The verse reminded my heart who hears me.

By the end of the week, my mornings had a softer edge. My thoughts were less tangled. My day still brought surprises, but I carried more peace into them. God was not far. He was first.

Prayer

Teach me to begin with You, not my phone. Set my ears to Your voice before the noise of the day. Help me prepare a simple space and meet You there with a quiet heart and open hands. Amen.

Practical Step

Create a tiny quiet-time tray with Bible, card, and reading glasses, and leave it on your spot.

"All Scripture is God-breathed... that the servant of God may be thoroughly equipped." – 2 Timothy 3:16–17

When I was younger, I felt pressure to read many chapters each day. If I missed a day, I felt behind. In retirement I tried the same approach and ended up skimming words that never reached my heart. It felt like eating in a hurry and forgetting the taste.

One morning I chose one verse. Just one. I copied it slowly in large print, the way a child traces letters. As my pen moved, the words settled. God breathed these words. They are not stale. They carry the warmth of His breath. The phrase "thoroughly equipped" caught me. Equipped for what? For the visits with my grandkids. For a hard conversation with a friend. For the quiet ache I carry on rainy afternoons.

I read the verse out loud. Then I circled one word and prayed it back to God. I pictured the verse like a seed planted, not a bouquet admired for a moment and tossed. Depth came from a single verse savored, not many verses skimmed. By lunch I found myself still holding that line in my mind, like a smooth stone in my pocket. It guided my tone, my choices, my rest.

I did not conquer a long list. I let one true sentence shape me.

Prayer

Breathe life through one verse today. Help me slow my eyes and open my heart. Equip me for the people and places I will meet. Let Your living word settle deep and bear quiet fruit that lasts through this day. Amen.

Practical Step

Choose one verse and copy it by hand in large print.

Week 4 — Pray Your Calendar

"Commit to the Lord whatever you do." – Proverbs 16:3

My planner used to boss me around. I wrote things down and then felt trapped by my own pen. Retirement softened the pace, but the tug remained. I still filled boxes without asking God what should fill me.

On Sunday afternoon I tried something new. I spread my week on the table. Appointments. Coffee with a neighbor. A doctor visit. A birthday. I placed my hands on the paper and prayed each line. Lord, this belongs to You. Interrupt as You wish. Protect my margin. Highlight what matters. As I prayed, I noticed a heaviness around one event. It was not necessary. It was there because I felt guilty saying no. Planning became worship when I surrendered before I started.

I crossed out that one item and felt lighter. Then I penciled in things that often get squeezed to the edges. A walk. A call to my sister. An hour to read the psalms. I left white space on purpose, like leaving room at the table for a guest. The week did not look empty. It looked open.

By Friday, two plans changed. Instead of feeling behind, I felt led. The calendar stopped being a master and became a map with prayer at the top.

Prayer

Order my steps and my stops. Teach me to give You my plans before I make them. Show me what to release and what to keep. Fill my week with Your priorities and Your peace, one decision at a time. Amen.

Practical Step

Lay your week's appointments before God, then cross out one non-essential item.

Week 5: Sabbath as Delight

"Call the Sabbath a delight." – Isaiah 58:13–14

It was Saturday morning, but my brain didn't know it. My mind was already in overdrive: laundry to fold, emails to answer, groceries to buy, a phone call to return, and the nagging sense that I was already behind. My coffee was still hot, but I was gulping it like a pit stop on a race track.

Then my daughter walked into the kitchen, her hair still messy from sleep, holding a puzzle box. "Will you do this with me?" she asked. My eyes darted to the clock. I had so much to get done before lunch. I almost said, "Maybe later," but something in her hopeful tone made me pause.

We cleared the table and opened the box. At first, my thoughts kept drifting to the sink full of dishes. But as we sorted edge pieces, I started to slow down. She giggled when I tried to jam the wrong piece into place. I smiled at how serious she looked when she finally found a match. Thirty minutes passed without me thinking once about my list. My heart felt lighter than it had in weeks.

That verse from Isaiah came to mind: Call the Sabbath a delight. I had always treated Sabbath as a religious obligation, something I was supposed to do. But in that quiet moment, I understood that Sabbath is God's gift, not His demand. It is permission to stop, to savor, and to remember that I am more than my productivity.

Rest is not laziness. Rest is trust in action. When I stop, I am saying, "God, You are still at work, even when I am not." That puzzle was not just a game. It was an act of faith. And faith, it turns out, is delight.

Prayer

Lord, teach me to see Sabbath not as a burden but as a blessing. Free my heart from hurry and give me courage to set aside my striving. Let my rest become worship and my joy become a testimony of Your goodness. Amen.

Practical Step

This week, set a two-hour Sabbath window. Put phones, planners, and to-do lists in a "Sabbath box." Fill that time with something that refreshes you such as walking, reading, creating, or connecting with a loved one without multitasking.

Week 6: Gratitude Rewires the Day

"Give thanks in all circumstances." – 1 Thessalonians 5:18

I woke up already behind. The coffee maker sputtered and died halfway through brewing. The weather app said rain all day, which meant my errands would be soaked. My phone had three texts before 8 a.m., all needing something from me. By 9:15, I had mentally labeled the day "a bad one."

Then I remembered something my friend told me: "Gratitude is attention, and attention is love." I decided to experiment. Instead of complaining, I would hunt for gifts in the very moments I disliked.

When the rain poured as I walked to the store, I noticed how fresh the air smelled. When the broken coffee maker forced me to stop at a café, I noticed the barista's warm smile and the cinnamon in my latte. When I sat in traffic, I noticed the red maple leaves glowing like stained glass in the drizzle.

By noon, my body felt different. My day was not suddenly perfect, but my attention had shifted. Gratitude did not erase the rain, the broken coffee maker, or the traffic. But it made me see the blessings woven into them. And when you see them, you cannot help but love the Giver.

Gratitude is a way of telling God, "I see what You are doing. I love it. I love You." It transforms a day not by changing the events but by changing the lens.

Prayer

Lord, open my eyes to the gifts I overlook. Help me train my attention to see Your hand in both the ordinary and the frustrating. Let gratitude be my default setting so my days are rich with Your presence. Amen.

Practical Step

Write down three specific thank-yous today. Include something you tasted, something you saw, and something someone said. Share at least one with a person who was part of it, whether by text, call, or face-to-face.

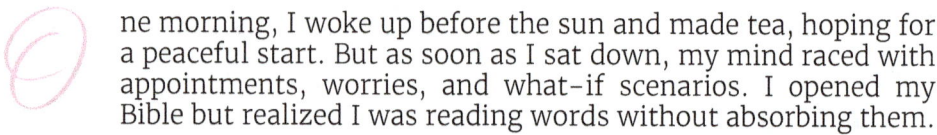

"For God alone my soul waits in silence." – Psalm 62:1

One morning, I woke up before the sun and made tea, hoping for a peaceful start. But as soon as I sat down, my mind raced with appointments, worries, and what-if scenarios. I opened my Bible but realized I was reading words without absorbing them.

So I closed my eyes. At first, the silence felt loud because my thoughts were shouting. But I remembered something I had once heard: "Silence does not mean nothing is happening. It means the noise is clearing so something can happen."

I slowed my breathing. Three long, slow breaths per minute. I pictured handing my worries to God like heavy packages. Slowly, the inner noise dimmed. Into that quiet came a verse I had not planned to read: "Be still, and know that I am God." My shoulders relaxed. The tea grew cold beside me, but my soul warmed with peace.

Silence is not empty. It is full of God. Worry shouts, but wisdom whispers. And whispers can only be heard in stillness. That morning did not solve my problems, but it reminded me that I am never alone in them.

Prayer

Quiet my restless thoughts, Lord, so I can hear Your whisper. Teach me to value stillness as the place where faith deepens and Your voice becomes clear. Amen.

Practical Step

Sit in stillness for three minutes. Slow your breathing to three deep breaths per minute. Do not speak, read, or pray with words. Just rest in God's presence and let Him speak in the quiet.

Week 8: Review and Reset

"Search me, O God, and know my heart." – Psalm 139:23–24

Life has a way of moving us on autopilot. We start strong with new habits such as more prayer, better boundaries, and intentional gratitude. Weeks later, our enthusiasm fades. I have learned that the key is not perfection but regular review.

One Sunday afternoon, I sat on the porch with my journal and read over the past month's entries. I noticed a pattern. My best days were not the ones with perfect schedules but the ones where I practiced Sabbath, gratitude, or stillness. I also saw the habits that were not helping, like scrolling late at night, which left me tired and irritable.

Review is like looking in the mirror. You can ignore the smudge on your face, or you can see it and wipe it clean. Reflection locks in learning, and reset keeps us moving forward.

David's prayer in Psalm 139 is bold: "Search me... test me... lead me." It is an invitation for God to show us what is working and what is hindering. The beauty is that He does not just point it out. He leads us into something better.

That afternoon, I chose one habit to keep, which was morning gratitude, and one to change, which was no screens after 9 p.m. Small steps can shift the whole path.

Prayer

Lord, shine Your light on my routines. Show me the habits that bring me closer to You and the ones that pull me away. Give me courage to adjust my rhythm so my life sings in step with Yours. Amen.

Practical Step

Look back over the last seven weeks of devotions. Circle one practice that has been most life-giving and schedule it again this week. Identify one habit that drains you and choose a small change to replace it.

Step 2 — Re-Anchor Identity in Christ (Weeks 9–16)

Your quick feedback is my blessing:

If this book has encouraged you or helped you feel less alone, would you leave a quick review?

Even one sentence makes a huge difference and takes just a minute.

As a small author, your feedback not only lifts my heart. It also helps other women of faith find the support and hope they need.

Thank you for being part of this journey!

Review Link Will be ready in 2 weeks, please be patientt... :(

Week 9: Beloved, Not Defined by Role

"I have called you by name, you are mine." – Isaiah 43:1

When I stepped into retirement, the air itself seemed to change. The pace of life slowed. No more Monday morning rush. No more urgent calls that pulled me in five directions at once. At first, I breathed a deep sigh of relief and thought, Finally, I can rest.

After a few months, the quiet began to feel less like rest and more like absence. For decades, I had been "the dependable one," "the organizer," "the teacher," "the go-to person." My days had been full of people and purpose. Suddenly, the phone barely rang, invitations slowed, and my calendar sat strangely empty.

One Tuesday morning, I sat at my kitchen table staring at the blank squares in my planner. A thought whispered in my mind that I did not want to admit: Who am I if I am not needed?

The question became sharper one afternoon at a luncheon. A friend began introducing me to someone new and paused. "This is… well… she used to…" Her voice trailed off while she searched for words. We both laughed politely, but inside I felt a sting. Used to what? Be important? Be relevant? Be worth knowing?

That night, I pulled my Bible from the shelf and opened it. My eyes landed on Isaiah 43: "I have called you by name, you are mine." It was as if God leaned in close and spoke directly to me.

He did not say, "You are mine when you are productive." He did not say, "You are mine when you hold a title." He simply said, "You are mine." My worth was never based on my role. It had always been rooted in His love, and that love had not shifted.

The next morning, I began a small habit. In my journal, I wrote my name followed by the words "God's beloved." At first, it felt awkward, as though I was trying to convince myself. But the more I wrote it, the more the truth began to settle deep. It was not a pep talk. It was a declaration of reality.

Over time, I began to see my days differently. My value was not in a busy calendar or in introductions that listed my achievements. My identity was secure, not because of what I did, but because of Whose I was.

If you have ever felt that your worth faded when a title or role changed, hear this. Roles shift, titles retire, seasons change. But "beloved" never expires. God called you by name long before anyone called you "teacher" or "manager" or "mom." That truth will never change.

Prayer

Lord, settle my worth in Your voice. Remind me that no accomplishment or title could add to or take away from the truth that I am Yours. Amen.

Practical Step

Write your name, then add "God's beloved" beside it. Place it in your Bible where you will see it every day this week.

Week 10: Strength in Weakness

"My grace is sufficient for you." – 2 Corinthians 12:9

A few months after knee surgery, I decided to rejoin my women's walking group. I had been looking forward to it for weeks. In my mind, I pictured myself keeping pace like I always had, enjoying laughter and fresh air with friends.

Reality was different. After just one block, my leg throbbed and my steps slowed. I told the others to go ahead and assured them I was fine, but inside I felt frustration rising. I had always been the one to help others, to carry heavy bags, to stay until the last chair was stacked. Now I could not even keep up on a neighborhood walk.

I sank onto a bench and tried to hide my embarrassment. As I sat there, a verse I had read so many times came to mind: "My grace is sufficient for you, for My power is made perfect in weakness." I had never liked thinking of myself as weak. Yet here I was, with no way to pretend otherwise.

When the group circled back, one friend slowed her pace and joined me. "Let's take the scenic route," she said with a smile. We walked slowly, and our conversation went deeper than it ever had when I was rushing ahead. My weakness had opened a door for connection that my strength might have kept closed.

That moment changed how I saw my limits. They are not always barriers to be overcome. Sometimes they are invitations for God to work in ways my self-sufficiency never allowed. They create space for others to serve me, which in turn deepens relationships. They remind me that I was never meant to live as if I could do everything alone.

You may not like admitting where you fall short. I do not either. But often, the very places we try hardest to hide are the places where God's grace shines brightest.

Prayer

Be strong where I am not, Lord. Let me see weakness as a place where Your power rests on me. Amen.

Practical Step

Name one limitation honestly to a trusted friend today.

Week 11: Refuse to Live in the Past

"Forgetting what lies behind and straining forward." – Philippians 3:13–14

We were cleaning out the garage when I found a dusty box tucked behind some old paint cans. Inside were photo albums, their covers worn from years of flipping through them. As I turned the pages, I saw birthdays, vacations, my children in caps and gowns. I smiled at the memories, yet a heaviness settled in my chest. Those days had been so full. Was the best already behind me?

That evening, the question stayed with me. Am I living in the shadow of what was? The Apostle Paul's words came to mind: "Forgetting what lies behind and straining forward to what lies ahead." Forgetting does not mean erasing. It means choosing not to let the past hold you back from what God is doing now.

God was not asking me to pack away the good memories or pretend that hard moments never happened. He was calling me to use the past as a foundation, not a cage. Gratitude can look back, but faith steps forward.

The next morning, I wrote down one regret that I had replayed in my mind for years. I prayed over it, thanked God for His grace, and then tore the paper into tiny pieces. It was a small act, but it felt like setting something free. Or maybe it was me who was being set free.

Your past can be a museum you keep revisiting, or it can be a launching pad into a future God has prepared. You get to choose which it will be.

Prayer

Help me release yesterday with gratitude, Lord. Free me from the weight of regret so I can run toward what You have next. Amen.

Practical Step

Write one regret on paper, pray over it, then tear it up.

Week 12: From Fear to Faith

"Do not fear, for I am with you." – Isaiah 41:10

When I was invited to speak at a women's retreat, my first instinct was to decline. The thought of standing in front of a group made my palms sweat. I began forming my polite excuse before I even finished reading the invitation.

That evening, I decided to at least pray before giving my answer. I opened my Bible and read Isaiah 41:10: "Do not fear, for I am with you." It felt like God was saying, "I will be there before you walk onto that stage." My fear had been shrinking my opportunities. What might happen if I stepped into the spaces God opened instead of stepping back?

On the day of the retreat, my heart raced and my hands shook. But as I began to speak, something shifted. My focus turned from myself to the women in front of me. The more I shared, the more peace replaced panic. I stumbled over a few words, but the message landed. Women came up afterward to say how it encouraged them.

That day taught me that God does not require flawless. He asks for faithful. Fear will always knock at the door, but when faith answers, the space you step into is often bigger than you imagined.

Prayer

Lord, trade my what-ifs for Your promises. Remind me that You walk into every room before I do. Amen.

Practical Step

List one fear, match it with a Bible verse, and post it where you will see it daily.

Week 12: From Fear to Faith

"Do not fear, for I am with you." – Isaiah 41:10

I used to think fear was something you either had or you did not. Brave people simply did not get scared. But fear is sneaky. It does not always look like trembling hands or racing thoughts. Sometimes it looks like procrastination, overplanning, or even a polite "maybe later" to things God has already invited me to do.

A few years ago, I was asked to lead a women's Bible study. My first thought was, What if I mess up? What if they think I am not qualified? I smiled and said I would pray about it, but the truth was, I was stalling. Every time the opportunity came to mind, my stomach tightened. The what-ifs began stacking like bricks, building a wall between me and the thing God wanted to give me.

One morning, as I read Isaiah 41:10, the words "I am with you" felt almost audible. It was as if God was saying, You are focusing on the wrong presence. You are imagining every fear in the room, but I will be in the room too. Suddenly I saw that fear was making the space smaller, when God had already opened it wide.

I said yes. And you know what? It was not perfect. I forgot a point, lost my place once, and my hands shook a little. But women shared their hearts. We prayed together. God moved in ways that had nothing to do with my performance and everything to do with His presence.

Fear tries to shrink rooms that God intends to open. It keeps us standing in doorways instead of stepping into the spaces He has prepared. Faith does not mean we will never feel afraid. It means we trust God enough to walk in anyway.

Prayer

Lord, trade my what-ifs for Your promises. Remind me You are with me in every room, every conversation, every step. Help me to see that fear is small next to Your presence. Amen.

Practical Step

Write down one fear that is holding you back. Find a Scripture that speaks directly against it, and post it somewhere you will see daily such as your fridge, WC mirror or phone background.

"Rejoice in the Lord always." – Philippians 4:4

I used to think joy would come when I reached certain milestones. I pictured it arriving in big celebrations, answered prayers, or special trips. Yet some of my most joy-filled days have not been flashy at all.

One Tuesday morning stands out. It was not a holiday or vacation. The laundry basket was full and my to-do list was longer than my patience. As I washed dishes, sunlight poured through the kitchen window and landed on the steam rising from my coffee mug. For some reason, that simple sight caught me. I stopped, closed my eyes, and thanked God for the warmth of the water on my hands, the smell of fresh coffee, and the sound of a bird outside the window.

Something shifted in my chest. My mood lifted, not because my circumstances changed, but because I noticed God in them. Joy is not something we stumble into by accident. It grows when we pay attention to the small ways God is already present.

Joy is not stored only in grand events. It lives in the ordinary moments we might rush past if we are not careful. When we choose to rejoice right where we are, the day becomes a gift instead of a grind.

Prayer

Lord, teach me to rejoice right where I am. Open my eyes to the small blessings that reveal Your goodness. Amen.

Practical Step

Take a ten-minute "joy walk" today. As you walk, thank God out loud for every small thing you notice.

Week 14: Wisdom for Decisions

"If any of you lacks wisdom, ask God." – James 1:5

I once spent two weeks trying to decide whether to take on a volunteer role. I asked friends for their opinions. I made pros and cons lists. I even researched time management tips to see if I could make it work. But I never actually stopped to ask God.

One evening, feeling stressed and still unsure, I opened my Bible to James 1:5. The words were clear. If I lacked wisdom, all I had to do was ask God. Not gather endless information. Not wait until I felt smart enough. Just ask.

So I prayed a simple prayer. Within the next day, I had a deep sense of peace about saying no to the role. The opportunity was not wrong, but it was not mine to carry in that season.

We often make decisions harder than they have to be. Wisdom is not a treasure hunt we have to navigate alone. God offers it freely when we pause long enough to ask.

Prayer

Lord, give me wisdom that is pure and peaceable. Teach me to come to You first before I act. Amen.

Practical Step

Before your next yes, pause and pray for one full minute, asking God for wisdom about the choice in front of you.

Week 15: Worth That Ripens with Age

"They still bear fruit in old age." – Psalm 92:14

There is a quiet pressure in our culture to measure worth by youth, speed, and productivity. I felt it when I left my full-time career and worried my most meaningful work was already behind me.

One Sunday, our pastor invited an older woman to share her testimony. She spoke of mentoring younger women, writing cards of encouragement, and praying daily for missionaries she would never meet in person. As she spoke, her eyes shone with life and purpose.

It struck me that she was not less fruitful because her pace had changed. If anything, her fruit was richer and more intentional. Age had not reduced her calling. It had concentrated it, like a tree producing its sweetest fruit in later seasons.

God does not retire His children from bearing fruit. He refines our purpose to match the wisdom, compassion, and faith we have gained over the years.

Prayer

Lord, let my later years be green with fruit. Show me the work You have prepared for me in this season. Amen.

Practical Step

Choose one younger woman to encourage this week. Send her a note, pray for her, or take her out for coffee.

Week 16: Abide to Bear Fruit

"Apart from me you can do nothing." – John 15:5

I am a list maker. Nothing feels better than checking off a completed task. But I have noticed something. The days when I jump into my list without spending time with God often leave me drained, even if I finish everything.

One morning, I was tempted to skip my quiet time because I had so much to do. Yet a gentle thought nudged me to open my Bible anyway. As I read John 15, the words about abiding struck deep. Fruit does not grow from a branch that works harder. It grows because the branch stays connected to the vine.

That day, I moved through my tasks with a sense of peace. Even interruptions felt less like obstacles and more like opportunities. The work still got done, but more importantly, my heart stayed close to Him.

Abiding is not a time slot on a calendar. It is an ongoing connection. When we stay with Jesus, fruit appears naturally, without striving.

Prayer

Lord, keep me close and fruitful. Teach me to remain in You no matter what the day holds. Amen.

Practical Step

Set a recurring daily reminder titled "Abide" at a time you often feel yourself drifting from God.

Step 3 — Renew Mind and Body (Weeks 17–23)

Week 17: Temple Care

"Your body is a temple of the Holy Spirit." – 1 Corinthians 6:19–20

*I*t was a Tuesday morning in March when I found myself staring at the pill organizer on the kitchen counter. Four different supplements sat untouched from the day before. Next to them was my Bible, still closed from yesterday. I had started the year with high hopes: early morning walks, more vegetables, a daily quiet time. Somewhere between endless phone notifications, late-night TV, and telling myself "I will start tomorrow," my temple had been neglected.

I was not sick or in crisis, but my energy felt like a leaking balloon. I started each morning fine, sagged by the afternoon, and was completely flat by bedtime. My prayer life had been reduced to whispered "help me" moments as I hustled through each day.

That verse about my body being the temple of the Holy Spirit floated into my mind, but honestly it felt like a guilty reminder, like a sticky note I kept ignoring. Until one evening, while folding laundry, I listened to a podcast where the speaker said, "Stewardship is worship in motion." She was not talking about money. She was talking about our bodies, our habits, and our everyday choices.

It clicked. God had entrusted me with this body, in this season. Not the one I had in my 30s, not the one I dream of next summer, this one. Taking care of it was not just self-help. It was worship. Every time I chose sleep over scrolling, water over soda, prayer over panic, I was saying, "Lord, I am grateful for what You have given me, and I want to use it well."

That night, I did not overhaul everything. I did not order an expensive smoothie blender or sign up for a marathon. I chose one small thing: walking for ten minutes after lunch. No excuses and no comparing to what I used to do. Just one habit, repeated.

Within a week, I noticed more than the physical change. Those walks became prayer walks. My body felt lighter, but so did my spirit. I realized I had been carrying the belief that temple care had to be dramatic to matter. In reality, faithfulness is built in tiny, consistent bricks.

Now, when I read that my body is a temple of the Holy Spirit, I hear invitation. God lives here. I can honor Him not with perfection, but with stewardship in motion.

Prayer

Lord, help me honor You with my habits. Teach me to see my daily choices as worship, and give me the wisdom to start small but stay faithful. Amen.

Practical Step

Pick one small habit to start or restart today, something you can realistically do every day this week.

Week 18: Contentment Now

"Godliness with contentment is great gain." – 1 Timothy 6:6

It happened at the farmer's market on a sunny Saturday. My tote bag was already full with fresh peaches, crusty bread, and flowers that smelled like summer. Still, I found myself eyeing the artisan pottery booth. The mugs were beautiful, earthy, and perfectly imperfect. I imagined how they would look on my kitchen shelf, how cozy my morning coffee would feel in one.

Then I thought about the cabinet in my kitchen. Behind the door sat eight mugs already. Some were gifts, some thrifted finds, some just because they were pretty. I did not need another. Still, the "but it is special" voice tried to make its case.

That is when the verse about contentment came to me. Not in a preachy way, but like a gentle nudge: Godliness with contentment is great gain. Gain meant more than I had now, not less. But the gain was not a mug. It was the peace of living within the lane God has me in right now.

Contentment is not a personality trait. It is a learned skill. Learning it means practicing it in tiny crossroads moments: walking past something that is fine to have but not wise to chase, saying "thank You" instead of "what else," breathing deep instead of filling the gap with more.

I smiled, thanked the pottery artist, and walked away with my tote bag exactly as it was. That decision did not change my shelf space, but it did make space in my soul.

When I got home, I made coffee in my favorite mug and felt that quiet gain. It was not about settling for less. It was about enjoying what I already had, knowing that gratitude always fills more deeply than grasping ever can.

Prayer

Lord, train my heart to say "enough" and mean it. Help me find joy in what You have given me, and keep me from chasing what will only clutter my soul. Amen.

Practical Step

List three things you will not chase this week. Thank God for what you already have in their place.

Week 19: Trade Anxiety for Prayer

"Do not be anxious… but in every situation, by prayer and petition, with thanksgiving, present your requests to God." – Philippians 4:6–7

I was standing in line at the post office, scrolling through my phone, when I realized my shoulders were up around my ears. My stomach felt tight. I had not even noticed the spiral. One news headline, a work email, and a text from a friend in crisis had me carrying a weight I did not remember picking up.

I thought about how often I do this: rehearse the problem over and over in my head, running imaginary scenarios like bad dress rehearsals for a play that never happens. Worry is just that, a rehearsal. But it is for the wrong performance.

Then the truth hit me. Prayer is also a rehearsal, but of God's presence, not my problems.

Right there in the post office, I put my phone away and took five slow breaths. On the inhale, I prayed, Lord Jesus. On the exhale, I prayed, I trust You. With each breath, the tightness loosened. My shoulders lowered. The knot in my stomach softened.

The problem was not magically solved. But my perspective shifted because my heart had shifted. Prayer had replaced the loop of fear with the loop of faith.

I have learned that trading anxiety for prayer is not a one-time event. It is a reflex you build. The more you practice, the faster the exchange happens. The more I rehearse God's presence, the more peace I feel.

Prayer

Lord, guard my heart and mind in Christ. Teach me to swap the habit of worry for the habit of prayer until peace feels like my natural state. Amen.

Practical Step

Worried? breathe in "Lord Jesus," breathe out "I trust You" five times.

Do it till you feel your body physically release tension.

Week 20: Simplicity Frees Attention

"Be content with what you have." – Hebrews 13:5

I opened the linen closet and a stack of towels tumbled out. Not because I had been careless, but because there was simply no room left. Some towels were faded, some never used, but I kept them "just in case."

That "just in case" thinking had crept into more than my closet. It had filled my calendar, my to-do list, and even my mind. I carried extras: commitments, possessions, mental tabs, until my soul felt just as cramped as that closet.

One afternoon, while I was shoving another blanket onto the shelf, I thought about how Jesus traveled light. Not just physically, but emotionally. He carried no grudges, no inflated social calendar, no storage bins of "maybe someday" projects. His hands were open, free to heal, touch, bless, and serve.

I realized that the clutter in my life was not just taking up space. It was stealing attention. Every extra item I kept meant one more thing to fold, store, clean, or think about. Every extra "yes" I gave meant one less moment of margin for God to use me in the unexpected.

That day, I filled one bag with towels to donate. It felt small, but it was a start. Every time I choose simplicity, I feel my attention loosen from things and land back where it belongs, on loving God and people well.

Prayer

Lord, loosen my grip on clutter in my home and in my heart. Free my attention to be fully present with You and the people You have given me. Amen.

Practical Step

Fill one donation bag today with items you no longer use or need. Let it be the first step toward a lighter, freer life.

"They shall run and not be weary." – Isaiah 40:31

I t had been one of those heavy weeks where even my morning coffee felt like it needed a nap. My calendar was packed with lunches with friends, volunteer meetings at church, babysitting the grandkids, and trying to tackle my ever-growing "to-do" list. Every day felt like a sprint, and by Thursday, I was running on fumes.

Friday morning, I sat at the kitchen table staring into my oatmeal as if it might magically hand me a second wind. My husband walked in and said gently, "You know, you do not have to do it all in one week."

I brushed it off with a smile, but inside, I felt the truth sting a little. I did not want to admit it, but I was rushing through life as if my worth depended on constant motion. It was not just physical tiredness. It was soul tiredness, the deep kind that no nap can fix.

That afternoon, I had a rare moment of stillness. The grandkids were napping, and the house was quiet. I picked up my Bible and it fell open to Isaiah 40. I have read it before, but this time the words about running and not growing weary caught me in the chest. They did not say, "If you try harder, you will not be weary." They said strength comes from waiting on the Lord.

Waiting was the very thing I had been avoiding. My days were so crammed that God barely got a word in. I realized I was like a phone that never got plugged into the charger. I kept trying to do more while my battery was flashing red.

That night, instead of rushing into chores after dinner, I put on my sneakers and asked my husband if he wanted to take a short walk. We strolled slowly, the summer air soft around us. We did not talk much, just listened to the crickets and the sound of our own footsteps. I could feel my shoulders drop, my breath deepen, and something in my spirit exhale.

It was not the walk that gave me new energy. It was the choice to pause and let God refill what life had been draining. I did not have to keep proving my strength. I just needed to receive it from the One who never runs out.

Prayer

Lord, I confess I often try to run without stopping to be with You. Teach

me to wait in Your presence so I can be renewed. Let my strength come from Your endless supply, not my own striving. Amen.

Practical Step

Schedule one short walk after dinner this week. Leave your phone inside. Let it be a time to breathe, listen, and let God refill your strength.

Week 22: Redeem the Time

"Make the best use of the time." – Ephesians 5:15–16

*I*t started with a simple question from my granddaughter. She asked, "Grandma, how long will you play with me before you have to work on your computer again?" My heart sank. I had not realized she noticed how often I glanced at my phone or slipped away to "just finish one quick thing."

That night, I replayed the day in my mind. I remembered how many times I had checked the clock, how often my hands were busy while my mind was somewhere else. My minutes were slipping through my fingers like loose change. I thought of the verse in Ephesians that calls us to make the best use of the time. The phrase "best use" made me wonder. Was I truly spending my minutes, or was I letting them scatter in pieces?

The next day, I decided to try something different. I blocked off one hour in the evening and put my phone in the kitchen drawer. My granddaughter and I sat on the floor with a puzzle. At first, I felt restless. My mind kept reaching for my phone. But then, something shifted. We laughed as we hunted for the corner pieces. She told me about her favorite part of school that week. That hour felt like it stretched and grew until it held more than sixty minutes.

By the time we finished, I realized something important. Minutes are not scraps we use up after the "real" work is done. They are seeds. When planted with purpose, they grow into memories, trust, and love.

I cannot go back and reclaim the time I have wasted, but I can choose to redeem the time I still have. It begins with being fully present for the people God has placed in my life today.

Prayer

Lord, teach me to number my days and fill my minutes with things that matter to You. Help me plant seeds of love and presence instead of letting my time slip away unnoticed. Amen.

Practical Step

Block one phone-free hour nightly for a week. Use that time to give full attention to one person or activity that matters most.

Week 23: Rest for Your Soul

"You will find rest for your souls." – Matthew 11:29

I used to think rest was something you earned. You worked hard, checked everything off your list, and then you could rest with a clear conscience. The problem was that my list never seemed to end. Even on my "quiet" days, I found myself cleaning closets, reorganizing drawers, or answering messages until bedtime.

One evening, I noticed my Bible sitting untouched on the coffee table. I picked it up and read the words of Jesus in Matthew 11. They stopped me in my tracks. He said, "You will find rest for your souls." He did not say, "You will finally earn rest after proving yourself." Rest, I realized, is not a prize for finishing the race. It is a gift for those willing to come to Him.

The next night, I tried something new. I turned off the television thirty minutes before bed. I made a cup of chamomile tea, wrapped a blanket around my shoulders, and sat in my favorite chair. I read a psalm slowly, letting each verse sink in. My breathing slowed. The knots in my shoulders began to loosen. I felt a peace I had not felt in weeks.

Rest was not something I achieved that night. It was something I received, like an open hand catching rain. My circumstances had not changed. The laundry still waited for me in the morning. But my soul had been calmed, not by my efforts, but by His presence.

Now I see that true rest is an act of trust. It is choosing to believe that God can hold the world together while I stop to breathe.

Prayer

Lord, I come to You for the rest only You can give. Quiet my heart, slow my thoughts, and help me trust You enough to stop striving. Amen.

Practical Step

Choose one soothing evening ritual and repeat it for three nights this week. Let it become a sacred space where you meet with God

and let your soul rest.

Step 4. — Clarify Calling and Purpose (Weeks 24–30)

Week 24: Seek First

"But seek first the kingdom of God and His righteousness, and all these things will be provided for you." – Matthew 6:33

The day started with my phone buzzing before sunrise. A text about a change in my doctor's appointment, an email from my daughter asking for help with the kids next week, and a group message about a community yard sale I had not planned for. Before I even made coffee, my mind was running through a list of errands, phone calls, and chores.

By the time I sat down with my Bible, it was nearly 10 a.m. and I was already tired. My prayers felt rushed, almost like a task to check off before getting to the "real" list of important things. Somewhere deep inside, I felt a whisper: This is why you feel scattered. You are starting with everything else.

That afternoon, I remembered a conversation with a friend. She had said, "If I do not put God first, He ends up last." It hit me that I had been doing the same thing. I wanted to trust God with my plans, but I kept inviting Him into my day after I had already filled it.

The next morning, I decided to test this verse in a practical way. Before I opened my phone, before the coffee, I sat in my favorite chair with my Bible. I read Matthew 6 slowly. It felt strange to let the laundry wait and the messages go unanswered for a while. But as I prayed first and planned second, my day seemed lighter. The appointments were still there, the chores still waited, but my heart was steadier.

I learned that "seek first" is not just a nice phrase for a Sunday sermon. It is a choice that changes the tone of the whole day. Order really does determine outcome.

Prayer

Lord, help me place Your priorities at the top of my list every single day. Teach me to trust that when I give You the first moments, You will guide everything else. Amen.

Practical Step

This week, schedule your church, small group, and serving dates before filling in anything else on your calendar. Let those be the anchors for your week.

Week 25: Gifts to Serve

"Each of you should use whatever gift you have received to serve others, as faithful stewards of God's grace in its various forms." – 1 Peter 4:10

When I first retired, I felt like my skills had an expiration date. I had spent years in an office, coordinating projects and solving problems. But who needs that in everyday life? I tried to fill my time with hobbies, but a quiet ache settled in. I missed making a difference.

One afternoon at church, a woman from our missions team asked if I could help with a fundraiser. "It is just making phone calls and keeping track of responses," she said. It sounded simple enough. By the end of that week, I had organized the list, followed up with donors, and found myself smiling in a way I had not for months.

The joy came from realizing something important: my skills were not gone. They had simply been waiting for a new assignment. The combination of my work experience and my personal faith was exactly what the ministry needed. That verse in 1 Peter became real to me. A gift is not meant to be shelved; it is meant to be opened again and again for the benefit of others.

Now I try to notice where my story and my skills meet someone else's need. It is not always in a big role. Sometimes it is helping with childcare during Bible study, other times it is proofreading the church bulletin. But every time, I feel that spark of joy.

Serving others with what you already know how to do is one of the most satisfying ways to live out God's calling. Your gift plus your willingness can become someone else's answer.

Prayer

Lord, thank You for the skills You have placed in my hands. Show me where they fit into the needs around me, and help me serve with joy. Amen.

Practical Step

Write down two of your skills or gifts. Email one ministry leader to ask how you can help in a small role this month.

Week 26: Mentor the Next

"Older women... are to teach what is good, so that they may encourage the young women." – Titus 2:3–5

I used to think "mentoring" meant being a professional counselor or a Bible teacher. I pictured a formal program with coffee meetings on the calendar and homework assignments. That is why I almost said no when a younger woman at church asked if we could get together to talk about life and faith.

We met at a little café. She had questions about balancing work, marriage, and spiritual growth. I told her about my own struggles when I was her age, including mistakes I wished I had avoided. I also shared how God had been faithful through every season.

By the time we finished our tea, I realized something. Mentoring is really about showing up and listening, then offering the encouragement and wisdom you already have. It is telling the truth about your journey, both the joys and the stumbles.

Over the next few months, our talks became a regular thing. We laughed about small frustrations, prayed about big decisions, and celebrated answered prayers together. I saw how much she grew, but I also noticed how much I grew. Sharing my life in this way reminded me of God's faithfulness all over again.

Mentoring is not about having all the answers. It is about giving someone else a living picture of what walking with Jesus looks like over time. Wisdom multiplies when it is given away.

Prayer

Lord, make me a gentle and faithful mentor. Give me eyes to see who needs encouragement, and the courage to share my story with honesty and love. Amen.

Practical Step

Invite one younger woman for tea this month. Listen to her story more than you talk. Pray for her afterward and check in within the week.

Week 27: Hospitality as Witness

"Share with the Lord's people who are in need. Practice hospitality." – Romans 12:13

Growing up, I thought hospitality meant a perfectly clean house, a three-course meal, and matching table linens. So when I became an adult, I avoided hosting unless I had weeks to prepare.

One winter, our neighbor lost power for two days after an ice storm. I invited her over for soup and bread. My kitchen table had mismatched chairs, and the soup was from a can, but we sat for hours talking about her childhood and her hopes for the future. That night, she told me it was the warmest she had felt in weeks.

It struck me that a meal does not have to be fancy to be holy. Sometimes, hospitality is simply creating space where someone feels safe and valued. A table can preach before a word is spoken. In that moment, my home became a place where God's love was quietly shared without a sermon.

Now, I try to keep a simple plan ready. Soup, bread, a clean spot at the table, and a listening ear. The focus is not on perfection but connection. Opening your door can open someone's heart to Jesus.

Prayer

Lord, open my door and my heart. Help me see opportunities to welcome others into a place where Your presence is felt. Amen.

Practical Step

Host a simple soup-and-bread night for two neighbors this month. Focus on listening to their stories more than impressing them.

"He has filled them with skill to do all kinds of work." – Exodus 35:31–32

I still remember the day my youngest granddaughter asked me, "Grandma, can you draw me a unicorn?"

Now, I am not what you would call a natural-born artist. My stick figures usually look like they are asking for help. But I grabbed a pencil and gave it a try. The result looked more like a tired horse wearing a party hat, but her eyes lit up like I had just painted a masterpiece. She ran off to show her mom, beaming, "Look what Grandma made!"

That afternoon, I thought about how much joy came from simply making something, even something imperfect. My hands had shaped a picture that carried love in every line, and somehow, that was enough. It reminded me of the verse in Exodus when God filled people with skill to build the tabernacle. Their work was both practical and beautiful. God did not just command them to throw up a tent. He gave them creativity as part of worship.

Somewhere along the way, I had let myself believe that creativity belonged only to "talented" people. But God made each of us in His image, and He is a Creator. That means creating is not just for the gifted. It is for the willing. Whether it is painting, gardening, sewing, writing, or baking bread from scratch, each act of creating is a reflection of His heart.

When I sat down later to try again, this time painting some flowers on a small canvas, I found myself praying as I worked. Every brushstroke felt like a conversation with God. I realized I did not have to wait until I was "good enough" to make something worth offering Him. He delights in the process, not just the polished product.

We live in a world that measures worth by likes, sales, or applause. The Kingdom measures worth by love, intention, and obedience. When we make beauty, even in small ways, we join God in His ongoing work of bringing life and light into the world.

If you have been holding back because you think you are not creative, I would challenge you to try again. Start small. Knit a scarf. Plant a pot of flowers. Write a poem. Even if it is messy or uneven, you may be surprised how much joy it brings, not just to others, but to you.

That unicorn drawing still hangs on my fridge. Every time I see it, I am reminded that God does not just give us breath to survive. He gives us hands to create.

Prayer

Lord, bless the work of my hands. Fill me with the courage to create with You, and remind me that my efforts, offered in love, are beautiful in Your eyes. Amen.

Practical Step

Start a small creative project this week and dedicate it with prayer. Even ten minutes of making something can be an act of worship.

Week 29: Pray for Your City

"Seek the welfare of the city… pray to the Lord on its behalf." – Jeremiah 29:7

One summer morning, I took my coffee outside and sat on the porch as the neighborhood slowly came alive. Mrs. Lesley was watering her roses. The twins down the street were racing their bikes. A delivery truck rumbled past, and the mail carrier waved. It struck me that I had lived here for years, but most of my prayers stayed inside the walls of my own home.

That week, I read Jeremiah 29:7. The people of Israel were in exile, far from home, living in a city they had not chosen. Yet God told them to pray for the place where they lived, even though it was imperfect. He told them to seek its welfare. If the city flourished, they would too.

I decided to take a prayer walk. At first it felt awkward. I was not sure what to say. But as I walked past the school, I prayed for the teachers and students. Passing the corner store, I prayed for the owner who always greets customers with a smile. At the park, I prayed for the children to grow up safe and loved.

Halfway down the block, I realized my prayers were changing how I saw my neighbors. It is easy to complain about traffic, noise, or politics. But prayer turns frustration into compassion. It shifts my focus from what I wish my city would be to what God can make it become.

Now, whenever I go for a walk, I take mental notes of what I see. The empty house that needs a family. The streetlight that flickers at night. The mom pushing a stroller while looking tired. Prayer does not have to be formal. Sometimes it is as simple as, "Lord, bless them."

God plants us in specific places for a reason. Your street, your apartment complex, your rural road… it is part of your mission field.

Prayer

Lord, bless my street and my leaders. Help me to see my city the way You do, and to pray with faith for the good You want to bring. Amen.

Practical Step

Walk one block this week and pray by name for what you see, whether it is a person, a business, or a need.

Week 30: Faithful Finances

"Honor the Lord with your wealth." – Proverbs 3:9–10

I used to think giving was something I would do more of "once I had enough." Enough savings, enough income, enough security. But "enough" always seemed just a little further away.

One year, during tax season, I came across a small line in my budget labeled "recurring gift." It was a monthly donation I had set up almost without thinking years ago. It was not much, just a small amount to a ministry I loved. I realized I had never missed that money, but over the years, it had quietly added up to something meaningful.

That moment changed how I saw generosity. Faithful giving does not start with extra money. It starts with a willing heart. Proverbs 3 reminds us to honor the Lord with our wealth, which means putting Him first, not just giving from the leftovers. When we give consistently, even in small amounts, it does more than help others. It loosens our grip on money and reminds us it all belongs to God anyway.

I started thinking of my budget as a tool for worship. Instead of just tracking expenses, I asked, "Does this spending reflect my values? Is it helping me live out my calling?" Those questions led to small adjustments. I canceled a subscription I barely used and increased my monthly gift by a few dollars.

The freedom came not from having more, but from knowing my money was working for eternal purposes. Generosity is not about the size of the gift. It is about the faith behind it. If money has ever felt like a source of stress or guilt, ask God to show you one step you can take toward faithful stewardship.

Prayer

Lord, make my budget a blessing. Teach me to honor You with my finances and to trust that You will provide as I give. Amen.

Practical Step

Set or adjust one small recurring gift this week, even if it is just a few

dollars, and pray over it as a seed for God's Kingdom.

Week 31: God Near the Brokenhearted

"The Lord is near to the brokenhearted and saves the crushed in spirit."
– Psalm 34:18

It was a Tuesday morning when I got the phone call. The kind of call that makes the world feel suddenly smaller and heavier all at once. My sister's voice cracked as she told me our cousin had passed away unexpectedly. I sat at the kitchen table staring at the mug of coffee in front of me, watching the steam fade, unable to take a sip. I felt like the oxygen had been pulled from the room.

The rest of that week blurred into phone calls, casseroles dropped off, and awkward hugs from people who wanted to help but could not fix what was broken. Nights were the hardest. When the house grew quiet and the distractions stopped, the ache came like a tidal wave. I could not understand how God felt close when I felt so alone in my grief.

One night, I could not sleep, so I opened my Bible without much thought. My eyes landed on Psalm 34:18. I read it slowly. "The Lord is near to the brokenhearted…" I sat with those words. Near. Not on the other side of my pain waiting for me to get better. Near, right here in the ache, steady in the silence.

It hit me that God's nearness is not reduced by loss. If anything, He leans closer. The pain did not disappear, but that night I pictured Him sitting with me at the kitchen table, not rushing me to feel better, simply steadying my breathing heart. And for the first time that week, I exhaled without crying.

Prayer

Lord, draw near to me in my grief. Help me breathe when my heart feels crushed, and remind me that Your presence is not afraid of my sorrow. Amen.

Practical Step

Write a two-sentence prayer of honesty about your pain. Read it aloud to God, knowing He hears every word without judgment.

Week 32: From Isolation to Belonging

"God sets the lonely in families." – Psalm 68:6

When my kids moved out, I expected the quiet in the house to feel peaceful. Instead, it felt hollow. The chairs around the dinner table were mostly empty, the phone rang less often, and my weekends stretched out like long, empty hallways. At first, I told myself it was just an adjustment. But over time, I stopped even trying to make plans.

One Sunday, a woman from church approached me with a bright smile. "We're starting a small Bible study on Wednesday nights. You should come." My first reaction was to make an excuse. It felt easier to stay home than to risk feeling awkward. But something in me knew God was nudging me.

That first night, I barely spoke. I listened to strangers share their struggles, their laughter, and their prayers. By the third week, someone asked how they could pray for me, and I surprised myself by answering honestly. Over the months, these people became more than acquaintances. They were the ones who brought soup when I was sick, who noticed when I was missing, who cheered me on in my faith.

Belonging had felt like something I had to work for, but I realized it was actually something God arranges when we step into the places H e leads us. He sets the lonely in families. Sometimes, that family looks like a circle of friends around a kitchen table with open Bibles and open hearts.

Prayer

Lord, lead me to safe and life-giving people, and give me courage to step into the spaces where You are setting me in community. Amen.

Practical Step

Choose one group, whether it is a church circle, hobby club, or service team, and attend once this week with an open heart to connect.

Week 33: Grieve with Hope

"We do not grieve as others do who have no hope." – 1 Thessalonians 4:13

When my friend Maria passed away, I thought I knew how to handle grief. I had been to funerals before, but this time felt different. We had shared so many ordinary moments—coffee on Tuesdays, grocery store runs together—that I could not imagine life without her. I cried until my head hurt.

At her memorial, I noticed something strange. Alongside the tears, there was laughter. People shared stories about Maria's joy, her quirks, and her stubborn faith. There was a light in the room that I could not explain. That night, I realized what it was: we were grieving with hope.

Hope did not erase the loss, but it changed its weight. It reminded me that death is not the end, that Maria is with Jesus, and one day we will meet again. That hope gave me permission to weep without drowning in despair.

In the weeks that followed, I created a small shelf in my living room. On it, I placed a photo of Maria, a card with her favorite Bible verse, and a candle. I would sit there for a few minutes some days, letting the tears come, but also whispering thanks to God for the hope that carries me.

Prayer

Lord, guard my hope as I honor my sorrow. Remind me that Your promises are stronger than death. Amen.

Practical Step

Create a small "memory shelf" with a photo, a verse card, or a keepsake. Spend three minutes there this week, praying and remembering.

Week 34 Friendship That Heals

"A friend loves at all times." – Proverbs 17:17

Last year, I went through a season when my health forced me to slow down. Doctor visits, physical therapy, and days of fatigue became my normal. One morning, I was feeling particularly discouraged when I heard a knock on the door. It was my friend Lisa holding two cups of coffee and a bag of warm muffins.

She did not ask if I wanted company. She simply came in, sat down, and listened. No fixing, no rushing, just presence. That day, I realized that friendship is not always about grand gestures. Sometimes it is about showing up when it would be easier to stay home.

Over time, I also saw how God uses friendship as a form of healing. Lisa's consistency reminded me that I was not forgotten. Her prayers for me gave me courage when my own faith felt thin. And in a quiet way, our friendship became a safe place for both of us to rest.

I used to think of friendship as a luxury. Now I see it as God's ordinary medicine for weary souls. Being a faithful friend is not just a blessing to others; it keeps our own hearts tender and open.

Prayer

Lord, make me a steady friend who shows up, and help me receive the kindness of others without pride. Amen.

Practical Step

Send a text to one friend today: "When can we walk and talk for 20 minutes this week?"

Week 35: Prayer Partners & Soul-Safe People

"Confess your sins to one another and pray for one another." – James 5:16

I used to think prayer was mostly a solo activity. My image of it was quiet mornings at my kitchen table, Bible open, coffee in hand, and no one else around. But there came a season when the weight of my thoughts felt too heavy to sort through on my own. I was showing up to church and smiling, but a friend noticed I was quieter than usual. After the service, she gently asked, "Do you want to pray together sometime?"

We began with just ten minutes on the phone once a week. At first, I was nervous. What if I could not find the right words? What if I cried? But I decided to try. I quickly learned that the power of praying with someone was not in saying everything perfectly. It was in being honest. I shared my struggles and fears, and she prayed right there for me. Then she shared hers, and I prayed for her.

That verse in James came alive. Confession is not only about listing our mistakes. It is about being willing to let someone else see the places where we feel weak, weary, or afraid. Prayer in that space becomes a lifeline. When you know someone is standing with you before God, you feel stronger and less alone.

Over time, our calls became a safe space. We celebrated answered prayers together. We listened with no judgment. We reminded eachother of God's promises when one of us felt shaky. Having that soulsafe space gave me courage and calm that I could not find by keeping everything to myself.

If you feel isolated in your prayers, find one trusted partner. Share openly. Pray together. You will be amazed at how much lighter your heart feels.

Prayer

Lord, give me one trusted partner to share and pray with. Help me be honest and willing to receive prayer as much as I give it. Amen.

Practical Step

Ask a woman to try a 10-minute weekly prayer call with you for a month.

Week 36: Healthy Boundaries, Gentle No's

"Above all, guard your heart." – Proverbs 4:23

When I first stepped into retirement, I thought I would have endless time for every request. If someone asked me to bake cookies, volunteer for an event, or watch their kids, I said yes. I liked being helpful. But slowly, I started feeling worn out. My schedule was packed, yet my soul felt empty.

One afternoon, I was rushing to finish a commitment I had agreed to even though I had not wanted to. I realized I had been saying yes to avoid disappointing people, not because it was right for me. The verse from Proverbs came to mind: guard your heart. That guarding is not about shutting people out, but about protecting the energy and focus God has given so we can spend them on what He truly calls us to.

Learning to say no kindly was not easy. At first, I felt guilty. But I began practicing one sentence: "Thank you for asking; I cannot commit to that right now." That sentence was short, kind, and clear. And each time I used it, I felt more peace. My yes began to mean more because I was no longer giving it away carelessly.

Boundaries do not limit love. They keep love healthy. When you guard your heart, you have more space for the people and purposes that matter most.

Prayer

Lord, teach me kind honesty without guilt. Help me protect my capacity for the right yes. Amen.

Practical Step

Write one sentence you can reuse: "Thank you for asking; I cannot commit to that right now."

Week 37: Courage for New Companionship

"Two are better than one." – Ecclesiastes 4:9

After years of a familiar routine, the idea of meeting new people felt intimidating. I had my friends, my habits, my comfortable spots in church and community events. But I noticed my circle was shrinking. Friends moved away, some became busy with family, and I found myself spending more and more time alone.

The thought of joining a new group made my stomach knot. I worried I would feel awkward or out of place. Yet the verse from Ecclesiastes reminded me that companionship is worth the effort. God designed us to walk with others, not just when it feels easy, but especially when we need encouragement and connection.

So I prayed for courage and signed up for a small group at church. The first meeting felt a bit uncomfortable. I did not know where to sit or what to say. But I introduced myself to two people and asked them about their week. By the end of the night, I felt a little more at home. A month later, I realized these were becoming my people.

New companionship does not replace old friendships. It adds fresh strength to your life. Sometimes God's next chapter for you begins with a simple hello.

Prayer

Lord, replace my fear with wise openness. Help me take the first step toward new connections. Amen.

Practical Step

Attend one new gathering, such as a small group, class, or volunteer shift, and introduce yourself to two people.

Step 6 — Bless Family and Community (Weeks 38–44)

Week 38: Bless Your Adult Children

"The Lord bless you and keep you." – Numbers 6:24–26

When my daughter moved into her first apartment, I felt both proud and nervous. Proud because she was stepping into adulthood with courage. Nervous because I knew how many practical details could trip her up. I started keeping a mental list of things to remind her about. Each time we spoke, I would weave in tips about checking her tire pressure, budgeting for groceries, locking her doors at night, and getting enough sleep.

At first, she listened patiently. She even thanked me for being so "helpful." But over time, I noticed her responses became shorter. Sometimes she would steer the conversation in another direction before I could finish my list.

One evening, I launched into a set of reminders about a work situation she had mentioned. I was halfway through when she interrupted me gently. "Mom, I love that you care. But sometimes I just need to hear that you think I am doing a good job."

Her words stopped me. I thought back to my own first apartment. I remembered calling my mother after a hard day, hoping for encouragement, and instead hearing a string of suggestions about what I could do better. She meant well, but I often hung up feeling like I was failing.

I realized I was doing the same thing to my daughter. Advice is important, but without blessing, it can feel like pressure. A blessing says, "I see you. I believe in you. I know God is guiding you." That truth opens hearts in a way instructions never can.

The next time we talked, I started differently. "I just want you to know how proud I am of you. You are handling this new season so well, and I can see God's hand on your life." Her voice brightened immediately. We ended up laughing together for nearly an hour. And without me prompting her, she asked for my thoughts on a challenge at work.

Blessing does not mean ignoring hard truths or avoiding guidance. It means building a foundation of encouragement so that guidance can be heard with an open heart. Our children, no matter their age, still need to know we believe in them.

When we speak blessing before advice, we mirror God's own heart. He calls us beloved before He calls us to grow.

Prayer

Lord, help me speak blessing before advice. Remind me that my words can either build walls or open doors. Give me wisdom to affirm the good I see and trust You to guide my children where my words cannot reach. Amen.

Practical Step

This week, send each adult child a short message of blessing. Be specific, such as: "I am proud of how you handled that situation. I see you growing, and I believe God is guiding you."

Week 39: Grandparenting on Purpose

"We will tell the next generation." – Psalm 78:4

My granddaughter was sitting at the kitchen table with a glass of chocolate milk, her feet swinging under the chair. She had just told me about a friend at school who was sad because her dad was sick. That reminded me of something from my own childhood.

I told her about the time my mother fell very ill when I was around her age. I had prayed every night for her to get better. Weeks later, she did. It was not dramatic like a movie, but I knew in my heart that God had listened.

Her eyes grew wide. "So God really heard you?" she asked.

In that moment, I understood the weight of what I was holding. This was more than a cute story from my past. It was a seed of faith I could plant in her heart.

Grandparenting is more than giving hugs, cookies, and holiday gifts. It is about intentionally passing down the stories that show God's faithfulness. Children may not remember every Sunday school lesson, but they will remember the personal testimonies of someone they love and trust.

I realized that I could fill her mind with more than just pleasant memories. I could give her a library of real-life examples of answered prayer, moments where God's hand was unmistakable, and situations where His peace carried me through.

These stories become more than history. They become anchors. When my grandchildren face storms in their own lives, they will have proof that God is real and active. And even if they forget the details, the memory of my faith will remain.

Being intentional means looking for everyday opportunities to connect their questions and struggles to God's care. It means speaking naturally about Him in a way that invites them to believe for themselves.

Prayer

Lord, help me be intentional with my words. Give me the right stories at

the right time to help my grandchildren see You clearly. Let my life be a living testimony that they can remember and trust. Amen.

Practical Step

Share one short story with a grandchild this week about a time God answered your prayer. Keep it simple and true, and invite them to tell you about a prayer of their own.

"If possible, so far as it depends on you, live peaceably with all." – Romans 12:18

I had once been close with a woman from my Bible study group. We often prayed together and shared meals with our families. But a misunderstanding over a small matter created distance. It started with short replies to text messages, then avoiding each other in the hallway at church.

I told myself it was better to stay quiet. I convinced myself that she should be the one to make the first move. But every time I prayed, her name came to mind. And each time, I felt God whisper, "So far as it depends on you."

One afternoon, I finally picked up the phone. My palms were sweating as I dialed her number. She answered cautiously, and I said, "I miss our friendship. I do not want this to keep us apart. Can we talk?"

Her voice softened instantly. She admitted she had been feeling the same way but was afraid I was still upset. That single phone call led to coffee together a few days later, and though our friendship took time to rebuild, the wall was gone.

Living at peace with everyone is not always possible. Some people will not respond. But God calls us to take the steps we can control. Peace often starts with one small act of courage.

If you are holding back because you are waiting for someone else to make the first move, remember that reconciliation is rarely about who is "right." It is about choosing unity over pride.

Prayer

Lord, give me courage to take the first step toward peace. Remove fear, pride, and resentment from my heart. Help me to be quick to forgive, slow to take offense, and willing to love even when it is difficult. Amen.

Practical Step

Reach out to one person you have been distant from. Whether it is a phone call, a letter, or a short visit, open the door for peace to begin.

Week 41: Cheerful Giver

"God loves a cheerful giver." – 2 Corinthians 9:7

A few years ago, I learned about a young single mother in our church who had lost her job. She was struggling to pay rent and put food on the table. My first thought was that I should help. My second thought was that my own budget was already stretched thin.

For several days, I wrestled with it in prayer. Each time, I sensed God nudging me to give, even if it meant sacrificing something on my end. Finally, I bought a week's worth of groceries and left them on her porch anonymously.

The next Sunday, she shared during our small group that someone had unexpectedly provided exactly what she needed that week. She wept as she told us how it reminded her that God saw her and cared. She had no idea it was me, and that felt exactly right.

In that moment, I realized that cheerful giving is not about recognition or the size of the gift. It is about letting God use you to meet someone else's need and trusting Him to meet yours.

Over time, I have noticed that giving with joy changes my own heart. It loosens my grip on money and deepens my trust in God's provision. And often, the joy I feel from giving far outweighs the cost.

Generosity is a way to join in God's work. When we give cheerfully, we reflect His nature. He is never reluctant to bless us, and He delights when we pass that blessing along.

Prayer

Lord, open my heart and hands to give with joy. Remove fear of lack and replace it with trust in Your provision. Help me to see giving as an opportunity to participate in Your love and care for others. Amen.

Practical Step

Choose one small but meaningful gift to give someone in need this week. Give it without expectation of thanks, and let the act itself be your joy.

Week 42: Guard Your Eyes and Mind

"I will set no worthless thing before my eyes." – Psalm 101:3

I used to tell myself that scrolling for a few minutes on my phone before bed was harmless. It felt like a small treat after a long day, a way to wind down. But one night, I realized something was changing in me.

It was late, and I had been flipping through videos and headlines for almost an hour. My mind felt restless. I noticed I was more irritable, less patient, and strangely unsatisfied. I was watching the highlights of other people's lives while mine was quietly passing by.

A few days later, I read Psalm 101:3, and the words felt like a direct message from God. "I will set no worthless thing before my eyes." It struck me that my screen habits were not neutral. The things I saw were shaping my thoughts, my mood, and my desires. If my eyes were the gateway to my heart, then I had been letting just about anything walk through the door.

That night, I decided to set boundaries for myself. I deleted a few apps that were the biggest time thieves. I put my phone in another room before bed. Instead of ending my day with noise, I picked up a devotional book and read Scripture until my mind felt peaceful.

It was not about being legalistic or fearing technology. It was about choosing what would feed my heart and mind. And over time, I noticed something beautiful. My sleep improved. My mornings felt lighter. My thoughts were clearer, and my prayers came easier. I was no longer drowning in meaningless input. Guarding what I set before my eyes was not about restriction. It was about freedom.

Prayer

Lord, help me set my attention on what is true, lovely, and pure. Give me the wisdom to guard my heart by guarding what I watch and read. Protect me from wasting my life on what does not matter. Amen.

Practical Step

Write a short personal media covenant. Include simple rules like when

to put your phone away and what you will no longer watch. Post it somewhere you will see it daily.

Week 43: Love Your Neighbor

"You shall love your neighbor as yourself." – Mark 12:31

When we moved into our current neighborhood, I had big dreams of connecting with the people around us. I pictured backyard barbecues, porch conversations, and helping each other with small acts of kindness. But as the years passed, I realized I had let busyness replace intentionality.

One Saturday morning, I saw my elderly neighbor, Mrs. Dawson, struggling to carry in her groceries. I waved and smiled but did not go over to help because I was "in a hurry." Later that day, I thought about how Jesus defined "neighbor" in Mark 12:31. It was not just the people we like or those we spend time with at church. It is literally the people God has placed near us, physically close enough for us to notice their needs.

The truth is, loving your neighbor is one of the most practical forms of ministry. You do not need a church stage or a mission trip to serve God. Sometimes, ministry looks like helping someone carry groceries, listening to a story on the porch, or simply learning a name and remembering it.

The next week, I knocked on Mrs. Dawson's door with a plate of cookies and a smile. We talked for over an hour. I learned about her late husband, her love for gardening, and how lonely she had been since her children moved away. I left feeling both convicted and joyful.

Loving my neighbor did not take a grand plan. It just required me to slow down, notice, and act. Geography really is ministry when we see it through the eyes of Jesus.

Prayer

Lord, help me see the people right in front of me. Give me a heart that slows down enough to notice their needs and courage to respond with love. Amen.

Practical Step

This week, learn the name of one neighbor you have never spoken to before. Ask them one question and listen closely. If possible, offer to pray for something they share.

Week 44: Encourage One Another

"Stir up one another to love and good works." – Hebrews 10:24–25

A few years ago, I received a simple handwritten note in the mail. It was from an older woman at church who had noticed that I seemed tired and discouraged. Her words were not fancy, but they were honest and heartfelt. She told me she was praying for me and reminded me that God was using my life in ways I could not see.

I read that note at least ten times. It felt like a breath of fresh air in a season when I was running on fumes. That one small act of encouragement gave me the strength to keep going.

Since then, I have tried to pay attention to the people around me who seem weary. Encouragement is like oxygen for courage. We often assume people know they are appreciated, but many do not. Sometimes, they are silently wondering if their efforts even matter.

When Hebrews 10 calls us to "stir up" one another, it is an active command. It means we take responsibility to help others keep going in love and good works. It can be as simple as a kind word, a listening ear, or a note in the mail.

Last month, I wrote a card to a young mom I know. I told her the ways I saw her loving her children well. When she thanked me, she said, "I had no idea anyone noticed." That reminded me again that encouragement is never wasted.

Your words may be the very thing that keeps someone from giving up today.

Prayer

Lord, help me be quick to speak life into others. Make my words a lift, not a weight, and give me the eyes to see who needs encouragement right now. Amen.

Practical Step

Write a handwritten note to one friend or family member who may be feeling weary. Mention something specific you admire about them.

Step 7 — Live Your Legacy (Weeks 45–52)

Week 45: Do Justice, Love Mercy

"Do justice, love mercy, walk humbly." – Micah 6:8

It happened in the middle of a church potluck. A dear friend had been treated unfairly by another member of our congregation. It was not just a misunderstanding. It was a wound that cut deep, and I could see the pain in her eyes every time the person's name was mentioned. She poured out the whole story to me one afternoon over ginger honey tea, her voice trembling with both hurt and anger.

Everything in me wanted to jump to her defense and label the other person as "wrong" so that I could neatly place them in a mental box and avoid them altogether. But that week, my Bible reading landed on Micah 6:8. I had read it many times, but the words "do justice" and "love mercy" stopped me in my tracks. I had always seen them as separate commands. One was about being firm, the other about being soft. Yet as I prayed, God showed me they were not meant to live apart.

Justice is about truth. It refuses to ignore wrongdoing. Mercy is about compassion. It refuses to reduce people to their worst moments. Justice without mercy becomes harsh and cold. Mercy without justice becomes careless and weak. When they work together, they reflect God's heart in a way nothing else can.

So I began to pray about how to live in that tension. I realized I could stand with my friend in her pain while still making space for the other person to repent and be restored. I wrote the person a short note, not to excuse the hurt, but to open a door for conversation. We eventually met. The conversation was hard, but it planted the first seeds of healing.

It was a reminder that a lasting legacy is often built in the way we treat those who have failed us. The choice to live with both justice and mercy may not be dramatic or noticed by the crowd, but heaven takes note.

Prayer

Lord, bend my heart toward justice and mercy. Teach me to stand firm in truth while walking in compassion. May I reflect Your heart in every relationship. Amen.

Practical Step

Pick one act of mercy this week and do it quietly, without telling anyone except God.

Week 46: Speak Blessing

"Gracious words are like honeycomb." – Proverbs 16:24

When my children were young, I often felt like a referee. There were toys to be shared, chores to be done, and squabbles to be settled. My words, more often than I liked, were corrective. I thought I was helping by pointing out what needed to change, but one afternoon I overheard my daughter say to her brother, "You always do it wrong." My heart sank. She was simply echoing the tone she had heard from me.

That Sunday at church, the pastor spoke about the power of words. He compared them to paint on the walls of a house. We can choose bright colors that bring warmth, or dull colors that make the room feel cold. Proverbs 16:24 describes gracious words as sweet and nourishing, like honey. I realized my words were not painting joy and hope in our home.

So I began a small experiment. Every morning, I looked for one thing to affirm in each family member. Sometimes it was as simple as, "I love how hard you worked on that," or "You make this home feel happy." The change was slow but steady. Laughter came back into our evenings. Conversations became more open. Even disagreements were calmer because the foundation of blessing was already there.

Speaking blessings does not mean ignoring problems. It means choosing to season correction with kindness so the truth can be received without crushing the spirit. Words are like seeds, and they will grow into something. The choice is ours whether they grow into weeds or fruit.

Prayer

Lord, season my tongue with grace. Let my words bring healing, encouragement, and joy to those around me. Amen.

Practical Step

Speak a short blessing at Sunday dinner over each person at the table.

Week 47: Pray Generational Prayers

"We have not ceased to pray for you." – Colossians 1:9–12

I can still see my grandmother at her small kitchen table. Her Bible was open, and next to it sat a worn spiral notebook. Inside were lists of names, dates, and handwritten prayers. She prayed daily for each one of us, her children, grandchildren, and even great-grandchildren she had not yet met. Whenever God answered, she would write the date next to the request in careful script.

After she passed away, I found that notebook tucked between her cookbooks. As I read through the pages, tears came. Some of the prayers had been answered years later, long after she had first written them. Many of the blessings in our family today could be traced back to her quiet persistence in prayer.

That notebook showed me that generational impact often happens in ways the world cannot see. Praying for the next generation is like planting oak trees. You may not sit in the shade yourself, but one day someone will. Our prayers outlive us because they are lifted to a God who is eternal.

I started my own prayer list for my children and grandchildren. Some prayers are for their character, others for protection, and others for opportunities to serve God with joy. Whenever I see God answer, I write the date. Over the years, those notes become a testimony of His faithfulness.

Prayer

Lord, grow wisdom, endurance, and a deep love for You in my family for generations to come. May my prayers prepare the way for their faith. Amen.

Practical Step

Start a one-page family prayer list and write the date beside each answered prayer.

Week 48: Finish What You Start

"I have fought the good fight... finished the race." – 2 Timothy 4:7

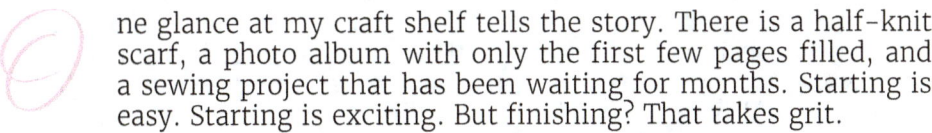

One glance at my craft shelf tells the story. There is a half-knit scarf, a photo album with only the first few pages filled, and a sewing project that has been waiting for months. Starting is easy. Starting is exciting. But finishing? That takes grit.

A few years ago, I signed up to coordinate a neighborhood food drive. The first week, I was enthusiastic. By the third week, I was tired, behind on my own chores, and ready to quit. But then I thought of Paul's words in 2 Timothy 4:7. He talked about finishing the race as a mark of faithfulness. It struck me that finishing is not just about completing a task. It is a form of worship.

When we finish what God asks us to do, we are telling Him, "You can trust me with what You give me." I decided to push through the final weeks of the food drive. It was exhausting, but on the last day, when we delivered the boxes to families in need, I felt a deep satisfaction. Not the kind that comes from checking off a list, but the kind that comes from obedience.

We live in a culture that celebrates beginnings with grand excitement. Heaven celebrates perseverance. The crown is not given at the start line but at the finish.

Prayer

Lord, give me the stamina to complete what You have placed in my hands. Help me finish with excellence and joy. Amen.

Practical Step

Choose one lingering task this week and block out two focused hours to finish it completely.

Week 49: Hope Over Fear

"May the God of hope fill you with all joy and peace in believing." – Romans 15:13

It was a gray morning in February, the kind that makes you want to pull the covers back over your head. I sat at the kitchen table with my lemongrass tea growing cold in my hands, scrolling the news headlines on my phone. Each story seemed heavier than the one before. On top of that, I had my own worries pressing in, questions about my health, concerns for my children, and an uncertainty about what the next few years would hold. The fear was not a sudden wave but more like a steady drip of water wearing away my peace.

I noticed I had been praying differently lately. My prayers had been short and anxious, as if I were handing God a list of things to fix. That morning, I set my phone down and looked out the window at the bare branches swaying in the wind. They looked so lifeless, yet I knew that hidden inside was the promise of spring. Even in the stillness, the trees trusted the seasons.

That is when the thought came: hope is not about wishing for the best possible outcome. It is about trusting the One who holds the outcome. Optimism tells me that things will turn out the way I want. Hope tells me that even if they do not, I am still safe in the hands of a faithful God.

So I prayed a different prayer that morning: "Lord, fill me with Your kind of hope—the hope that does not depend on my circumstances but on Your unchanging nature." The fears did not vanish instantly, but something in me shifted. My shoulders relaxed. My heart steadied. And I knew that hope had begun to grow again.

Prayer

Lord, fill me with a steady and believing hope that rests in who You are, not in what I see. Let my heart be anchored to Your faithfulness so that fear loses its power. Amen.

Practical Step

Write down three fears you are carrying right now. Next to each one, write one truth about God's character that speaks to it. Keep this list somewhere you will see it often this week.

Week 50: Remember and Give Thanks

"Forget not all his benefits." – Psalm 103:2

The week after Christmas, my house felt strangely quiet. Wrapping paper was gone, the decorations were coming down, and I sat staring at the empty calendar for the new year. Instead of excitement, I felt tired and uncertain about what was ahead.

I pulled out my old journal and flipped through the past twelve months. At first, all I noticed were the hard parts: prayers still unanswered, disappointments I had carried, and unexpected turns I had not planned for. But as I slowed down, I saw what I had nearly forgotten. A neighbor had shoveled my driveway after a snowstorm. A letter from a friend arrived at just the right moment. An unexpected financial gift came when bills were stacking up.

The more I read, the more I realized the year had been marked by God's kindness. I had been too burdened to see it clearly, but gratitude began to rise in me like a candle pushing back the dark.

I decided to make a one-page list of His benefits. I wrote down every answered prayer, no matter how small. I added the moments of peace in uncertainty, the laughter that came when I least expected it, the reminders that I was not alone. By the time I finished, I felt lighter. My circumstances had not changed, but my heart had. Gratitude had filled my year with joy.

Prayer

Lord, thank You for the quiet miracles, the big rescues, and the everyday mercies that I too often forget. Help me keep a heart that notices and remembers. Amen.

Practical Step

Create a one-page "year in review" listing answered prayers, moments of joy, and unexpected blessings. Keep it somewhere visible as a reminder for the months ahead.

Week 51: Open Hands

"Whoever refreshes others will be refreshed." – Proverbs 11:25

The guest room closet was overflowing. I had been meaning to organize it for months, but each time I opened the door, I quickly shut it again. One Saturday afternoon, I finally pulled everything out into a giant pile on the bed.

As I sorted through the blankets, kitchen gadgets, and clothing, I realized that many of these items had not been used in years. Some still had tags on them. I told myself I was keeping them "just in case" but deep down I knew I was simply holding on.

Then I remembered a time years ago when a friend had given me something I needed, no questions asked. The joy I felt in receiving it was so strong that I still remembered it clearly. I wondered—when was the last time I had been that kind of blessing for someone else?

That afternoon, I set aside three good things I had not used in a year. I gave one to a young mom in my church who was starting over, another to a neighbor who had admired it months ago, and the last to a local shelter. Each time, I saw a smile spread across their faces. I realized that giving did not just bless them; it refreshed me too. My heart felt lighter. My home felt freer. My faith felt stronger.

Generosity is not about how much we have, but about trusting God enough to live with open hands.

Prayer

Lord, keep my heart and my hands open. Help me to live generously, trusting that You will always provide for my needs. Amen.

Practical Step

Choose one good thing you own but do not use and give it away to someone who could truly enjoy it.

Week 52: Behold, He Makes All Things New

"Behold, I am making all things new." – Revelation 21:5

New Year's Eve has always been a mix of emotions for me. There is joy in looking forward, but also a hint of sadness as another year closes. Last year, I sat by the fireplace with my Bible open, reflecting on all that had happened.

When I read the words in Revelation—"Behold, I am making all things new"—I paused. These were not just words for the end of time; they were a promise for today. God is not only preparing a new heaven and earth, He is also renewing our hearts and our lives right now.

The more I thought about it, the more hope I felt. One day, there will be no more pain, no more tears, no more loss. That truth changes how I see the present. I can face the year ahead knowing that even the hardest moments are not the final chapter. I can forgive freely because ultimate justice is in His hands. I can love deeply because love will never be wasted in His kingdom.

So I decided to mark the turning of the year in a different way. I planned a small gathering with family. We prayed together, read Revelation 21:5 aloud, and dedicated the next year to God. It was simple, but it felt sacred.

Prayer

Lord, fix my eyes on the promise of Your new creation.
Let that hope shape how I live, love, and believe today.
Amen.

Practical Step

Plan a simple New Year's celebration. Read Revelation 21:5 aloud and pray together, dedicating the year ahead to God's purposes.

"Let us hold unswervingly to the hope we profess, for he who promised is faithful." – Hebrews 10:23

You have reached the end of the year's journey. Maybe you read every single week as planned. Maybe you missed some and doubled up later. Either way, you have been taking steps toward a more peaceful, prayerful, and purposeful home.

Peace rarely arrives with a loud announcement. Often it grows quietly. You may not notice the change in the moment, but it shows up in how you respond when the day unravels, in the tone you use with your children or grandchildren, and in how you steady your home when challenges come. Hope teaches your voice to soften. Gratitude slows your reactions. Open hands make space for love. Trust keeps you calm when answers take time.

This book does not have to be finished and forgotten. You can repeat your favorite weeks. You can revisit certain themes during new seasons of life. The lessons remain useful year after year because God keeps meeting you where you are.

Carry It Forward

Keep setting aside three minutes each week for reflection, prayer, and one simple step.

When life changes with new challenges or new opportunities, go back to the weeks that speak into your season.

Start a Family Blessing Ritual

One of the most powerful habits you can begin is reading a short blessing over your family every Sunday night. It can be a verse, a brief prayer for the week ahead, or a simple statement such as, "May the Lord bless you and keep you this week," planting seeds of security, peace, and love in your home. Your race is not run in one day but one faithful step at a time, so keep showing up, keep praying, and keep building on the foundation you have laid this year as I work on the next book with more lessons and devotions to help you continue this journey.

*I*f this book has helped you, it would mean so much if you'd leave a review. I read every single one, and your words help other women find the support they need on their own journey.

"Therefore encourage one another and build each other up, just as in fact you are doing."
— 1 Thessalonians 5:11

Consider picking up a few extra copies for friends... sometimes the people in our lives need these tools too, or simply want to understand you better. Who comes to mind? Write the names of people you can gift this book to, to enhance their lives and yours:

People who could use this book:

....
....
....
....
....

More resources and books are on the way... this is just chapter one of a story we'll write together. Thank you for letting me walk beside you. I'm cheering for you always!

With love,
Esther <3

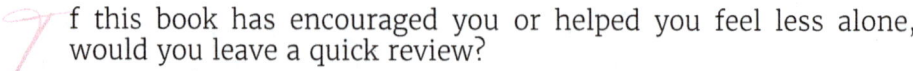

Your quick feedback is my blessing:

*I*f this book has encouraged you or helped you feel less alone, would you leave a quick review?

Even one sentence makes a huge difference and takes just a minute.

As a small author, your feedback not only lifts my heart. It also helps other women of faith find the support and hope they need.

Thank you for being part of this journey!

Review Link will be ready in 2 weeks, thanks for your patience